THE BLACK MAN'S
GUIDE TO WORKING IN A
WHITE MAN'S WORLD

By E. LeMay Lathan

Publisher: W. Quay Hays
Designer: Chitra Sekhar

For information:
General Publishing Group, Inc.
2701 Ocean Park Boulevard
Santa Monica, CA 90405

Library of Congress Cataloging-in-Publication Data

Lathan, E. LeMay
    The black man's guide to working in a white man's
world / E. LeMay Lathan
    p.   cm.
    ISBN 1-57544-051-2
    1. Vocational guidance—United States. 2. Afro-
Americans—Employment. I. Title.
    HF5382.5.U5L32 1997
    650.14'089'96073—dc21   97-11881
                                             CIP

Printed in the USA by RR Donnelley & Sons Company
10 9 8 7 6 5 4 3 2 1

General Publishing Group
Los Angeles

Contents

Dedication

To my son—for a better life for him; To my wife—for her inspiration and confidence in me; To my mother and my stepfather—for their love and devotion; To my mother-in-law—for her helpfulness and unselfishness; and most of all, to the memory of my Great-Grandmother and my Grandmother—for without their lessons and love there would be no me.

Letter to My Son

Dear Marcus,

From the moment you were born, your mother and I have wanted only the best for you. Our sunny dreams are often clouded by the realization that many challenges will confront you, just as they will each and every young person growing up in America today. As much as we'd like to shelter you from unpleasantness, we're equally committed to instilling in you a strong sense of family, of community, and of the realities of working in the white man's world. Believing that preparation is the key to success, we want to arm you with a sense of right and wrong, a solid education, the courage to take risks and make choices, and the understanding that motivation and hard work will help you realize your dreams.

I've worked hard to realize my American dream, and I did it by mastering the Game. That's all it really is—just a game. There are

5

winners, and there are losers. I'll never be able to answer all of your questions as you prepare to play the Game, though I can offer to share my experiences, my knowledge, and my winning strategies. Being successful in my career has allowed me the freedom to live the life I'd envisioned for my family and myself. Though you're just beginning life, the lessons I offer you and others in this guide are timeless. The rules may change and the playing field may become unrecognizable, but working in the white man's world will always be a game. And learning to play is the key.

All I can ask is that this guide be read with an open mind. You can be anything you want to be if you're willing to work hard enough. The world awaits you.... Be ready.

Your loving father,

Eugene Lathan

Introduction

The fact is, America is a white man's world, and the white man will never give up the world he has worked so hard to advance. It is futile, foolish, and pitifully stupid for us to sit around and think we are "entitled" to something that has never been ours in the first place. Use logic. If blacks had control of life in America, would we relinquish it to someone else? No way! The reality is, no one is going to hand the good life to us. If we want to win anything, we have to play the Game.

The Black Man's Guide to Working in a White Man's World is essentially an inside look at the nation's workforce and how blacks have and haven't fit in to it. But listen, my brother, it is also a statement about living well—the

7

challenge of making life work for us in this white man's world.

Many black men think of their existence as a struggle against the white man. This view is sometimes supported by well-meaning academics as a way to understand the past, or as an excuse to put present social problems such as poverty, crime, and unemployment into context. Unfortunately, it has also become the crutch of countless members of various oppressed groups who resort to what I call "the blame game" in their efforts to define themselves. For the good of the race, I suggest we stop blaming the white man for our contemporary hardships, and take responsibility for our lives and our futures.

So I've written this book because it needs to be written. I pull from my own experiences, with little regard for today's preoccupation with political correctness. I discuss why it is crucial that the black man change his situation himself rather than wait for white America to give him his "due." I criticize the liberal political agenda that actually enables my race to remain downtrodden despite its claims to the contrary. And I reflect on my hopes for the future of the black race.

The Game

The black man must play the Game. Even

though we didn't design it, we must understand its rules and abide by them. To reach the American dream, we must look to those who have already attained it by playing the Game, and emulate their strategies.

The Workplace

Until you start your own business, chances are you'll be working for the white man. Black people must try to focus on three thoughts throughout the workday: Do the best we can. Improve our skills. Add to our professional credentials.

The Players—Us and Them

Generally speaking, white kids are taught from the beginning that education is needed to succeed at the Game. Black kids, on the other hand, often witness a mother—or sometimes both parents—not working, or working hard but barely earning enough to get by. It is not the white man's fault, it is not the government's fault—it is the fault of today's black parents who choose not to explain why they have dead-end jobs, why they didn't provide themselves with the proper education and training, why they never learned to play the Game. Black parents must stop giving the impression that the blame lies with someone else.

9

Preparation

Liberals proclaim, "We have to save the kids now," but I don't wish to try to save our youth in the same way they do—through social programs, lenient rulings, or government handouts. Instead, we must prepare our young for adulthood by teaching them to be contributing members of society, and we must lead by example.

Education, of course, is the key. But it doesn't stop with just good grades and books. I'm concerned about the values and the morals that we teach our children—or don't. If we are undereducated in any or all of these aspects, we remain underprepared to enter the workforce. And that makes the Game all the more difficult.

Attitude

The black man says he wants to build a strong race but resents any suggestion that sounds to him like the white way of doing things. But use common sense—we rob one another, abandon one another, kill another in alarming proportions; we are destroying our own race from within. Whites don't do this, and their race stays stronger. Attitude is everything, and the black man must shed his hatred for the white man, and allow himself to learn from the white man if the black race is to endure.

Community

Black adults must prepare young blacks so that they are more equipped to compete. Black adults must change their attitudes about how one gets ahead and stop uselessly resenting the white man for what his forefathers did to ours. We must no longer live in the past. We must instead put community first, and eliminate those problems such as gangs and drugs that hurt our image and, more important, the quality of our present lives.

Political Agendas

We want elected officials to solve our social ills, but we won't show up at the polling booth on Election Day. This is another example of how we want to beat the white man without playing the Game.

I question whether the influence of liberal programs and policies has been of any genuine long-term benefit to the black man. Widespread abuse of welfare has drained the nation's taxpayers and created a generation of dependent minorities who have no clue how they'll survive if the program is modified or cut altogether. Many elected black officials have successfully managed to funnel government dollars into black neighborhoods, but have not sought to change the attitudes of their constituencies. I maintain that it doesn't matter how many jobs you create for blacks if the blacks don't want them, or how many neighborhoods we clean up if their inhabitants won't keep them that way.

The Future

I warn you that my words are often taken as an affront to the black race. No malice is meant; my heartfelt concern is for the good of the race.

I dislike the accusation that I am just trying to be white. I'm a black man and I can never change the color of my skin. I just cannot bear to go on seeing things stay the same—we are destroying our own neighborhoods, our own families, our very race.

I want the struggle to end. I want the black man to blossom and get from life all it has to offer. I want America to be the truly equitable nation that I know it can be, in which the American dream is attainable for each and every citizen.

If you want to beat the white man, the only way to do it is to play the Game.

The thoughts I have put on these pages have come from my heart and my real-life experiences. I have been working in the white man's world for nearly 20 years. In every job I have been either the only black person or the only black person in a supervisory position. I've received resentment from white subordinates and have been called an Uncle Tom by blacks. Through it all I've always returned to one thought—that I was hired to do a job and work with people, not make friends. I've mastered the Game.

Chapter One

Hard work spotlights the character of people: some turn up their sleeves, some turn up their noses, and some don't turn up at all.

—Sam Ewing

14

How I Won the Game

Get motivated to participate in the Game and learn all you can from those who have mastered it.

You can earn your piece of the American dream—a secure family life, personal satisfaction, and professional opportunities. No one is going to hand you something for nothing; it is entirely up to you.

15

T he working world is a game, and the most important things you need to know when playing any game are its object and its rules. The Game is simply the American way of life, the golden dream, the ultimate opportunity. A secret to getting ahead in the Game is to play it as the people who are winning play it. We already made our mistakes, so you might as well learn from them, too. Here's the path I took, mistakes and all, to get ahead in the white man's world.

One thing I learned early on is that until you develop the motivation, you can never compete in the Game. Whether it's a secure family life, personal satisfaction, or professional satisfaction, the motivation has to come from you. Motivation is the key to everything, and this guide is for black people who have or can find this motivation. You provide that—and I'll tell you the rules.

17

I first understood my motivation when I was growing up in inner-city Mississippi (if there is such a thing), watching the television shows popular at the time, such as *Leave It to Beaver, The Dick Van Dyke Show,* and *The Andy Griffith Show.* These were the shows that I thought depicted so-called middle-class American life, the life I wanted for my family and myself, the life that I think everyone wants.

But at some point the black man loses this dream. I almost lost mine many times. My life was nothing like the lives of those characters on television. The family unit was not the norm in my neighborhood. Single-parent homes with four or five children were what I was used to seeing. I was raised by my great-grandmother, who fortunately taught me the morals and values of her generation, not the values that were current. I didn't understand why her teachings made no sense. It wasn't until much later that I saw that what she was teaching me came from a different time, a different mind-set, a different America.

I had no one to educate me in how to live in the two-parent family unit except the television shows I watched. I thought all white people lived the way they did on television: Dad went to work to make the money, and Mom took care of the kids and the home. I wondered why there were so few black families living like this. So many times I was told that it was only television, and that if any people lived this way at all, only white people did. "Don't rot your brain with that white man's bull; life doesn't work like that for us" was what I was often told as the television was turned off and I went outside to play.

But my dreams began when, as a child, I saw a new way of life that was lived on television. I didn't map out my own life, but lived it day by day, as did many black people at the time. Yet I never lost sight of the future— my future.

I initially encountered the Game when I sought my first job after being discharged from the Navy. I had experience working in self-contained power plants, but found that people in the private sector were not willing to give me a job doing what I knew. I still needed to pay my bills and eat, so I had to have some way to produce an income while I applied for the positions for which I was qualified. As I began to interview for available positions, I found out just how underqualified I was and how many others were looking for the same positions. It was clear that I had to go back to school or look to another field.

I took a job as a security guard at a cemetery. My duties consisted of an hourly survey

19

of the site, checking the locks on all buildings and securing entrance gates, and reporting the status to the central office. My work hours were from 4 P.M. until midnight, Monday through Friday. As you may have noticed, my first job wasn't that of company president or CEO. It was an entry-level job. When I started, I didn't see myself doing this job for the rest of my life. I saw it as a stepping stone. Remember, this was my first job out of the Navy. I had had only military experience and a high school education.

As I began to interview for available positions, I found out just how underqualified I was and how many others were looking for the same positions. It was clear that I had to go back to school or look to another field.

I had made the mistake of not continuing my education. Don't allow this to happen to you. As the months passed, I applied for more and more jobs in many different fields, finally landing one as a driver for a computer-disk company. Since my security guard job was at night and the driver's job was from 7 A.M. until 3:30 P.M., I had just enough time to get from one job to the other. Working both did two things for me: it gave me additional income (which I had no time to spend), and it kept me from having idle time to cause or get into trouble. Again, I saw no reason to return to school, as

20

I had enough money to pay my bills and buy what I needed. This seemed to work so well that I actually attempted to work three jobs, applying for and getting one as a security dispatcher at a hotel.

I was able to hold three jobs by working my daytime driver's hours, then at the hotel from 4 P.M. until midnight, Monday through Friday. On Saturday and Sunday, I worked double shifts at the cemetery. With this arrangement, I was able to work 112 hours a week: 16 hours a day, seven days a week. I had absolutely no time to spend any money and no time to rest between jobs. I averaged about $550 per week, and, as this was in the late '70s, $2,200 a month was decent money. Still, working three jobs with little time in between was not tolerable for long, and this situation lasted only for about six months.

After that, things started to go bad. The security guard job became a pain because I was hearing about the fun my friends were having on the weekends, so I decided to give up that job and have my weekends free. I thought that if I relied on my savings and continued to work two jobs I'd be fine. But I didn't anticipate that the hotel would cut back and eliminate my security dispatcher job. With only one job to support myself and plenty of free time to party with my friends, my savings seemed to disappear a lot faster than I'd expected. Then I got the worst news of all: the computer-disk company had lost some big clients and no longer needed two drivers. You know the old saying LAST HIRED, FIRST FIRED. Now I was faced with no job, dwindling savings, and few prospects. But I knew there were still silver linings in all the dark clouds above me. After all, this was still America. And my dreams were still alive.

I began my search for another job but still felt no urgent need to return to school. I thought I could get a job or two and make a pretty good living. Again, I made the mistake of not looking to education as an option. I still hadn't figured out that I was just looking for a job to maintain the life I had as opposed to educating myself and looking for a career to start the life I believed was out there for me. I think I knew deep down that I needed to return to school, but I just wasn't willing to put aside the fun to make that possible. So the job search continued. After applying for several and having some interviews but no callbacks, things began to get desperate.

Then, in the classified ads, I read: WANTED, WAREHOUSE WORKERS, NO EXPERIENCE NECESSARY. Just what I was qualified for, so off I went to apply. Turns out it was a temporary agency with a contract to provide labor for a company to set up appliances and furniture in new apartments. I took the job. The first assignment lasted only four days. On the fifth day, my personnel manager called and asked if I would be interested in working in the stockroom at a hospital for about two weeks. At first I was pleased, until he told me where the hospital was located. I was going to have to drive 60 miles round-trip every day for two weeks. But I was determined to do what it took to survive, so I took the assignment. This turned out to be the job for me. There was no way I could have known it at the time, but I took the chance. You have to take chances in life. You may not always get the results you want, but the one chance you decide not to take could turn out to be the one that could change your life.

I was quite pleased with the way things were going. I had a job that would last two weeks. Then, the department head told me that the person whose job I was filling had decided not to come back to work, and asked if I was interested in the job.

I said yes right away, never stopping to think about all the driving back and forth the job required. I ended up working for this hospital for the next seven years, three of which I was the receiving and stockroom supervisor. This job was good for me, and I was good at it.

Liking the job and the people I worked with helped. I took my time and learned everything I needed to know to do an excellent job. I also found out what my next step up the ladder should be: to become a buyer. So I grilled the department head about how to prepare for the position and asked if there would be an opening anytime soon. The department head told me, "I wouldn't even recommend you for a buyer's position." I was in such shock that I couldn't even ask why. I just returned to my work and wondered what I had done that would make him not recommend me. I can't remember ever thinking that my race had anything to do with it.

But this was just the thing I needed to get my motivation back on track. His statement made me so mad that all I could think of was leaving. It finally began to dawn on me that controlling my future depended on my returning to school. I knew that motivation had to be my own. I had never lost my motivation, but I hadn't yet taken the right road to succeed.

I made the right choice this time to return to school and get the education I should have gotten in the first place. I realized my life could have been a lot different and maybe a lot easier had I pursued an education at the outset.

I continued working at the hospital, with no change in my attitude or work habits. I still arrived early and left late. Meanwhile, I enrolled at the local city college with the guidance of a VA counselor. After some discussion, I decided that solar technology was the most up-and-coming field to enter. As my classes started, I was elated with the instructors and the curriculum. All went well, until my second semester. The class was Introduction to Mechanical Drafting. From the first day, I knew that it and not solar technology was the field I should pursue. The next step was to try to change my major to mechanical design. But my counselor didn't agree with the change and wasn't willing to help me. So I went to another counselor and explained the situation and the change I wished to make. This too proved to be of no help.

Then I made the difficult but important decision to leave city college and pursue my field through a technical trade school specializing in mechanical drafting and design. I don't recommend this road for everyone, but I had a strong feeling that this was the field for me. It took long, hard thinking and many conversations with people I trusted to make the decision.

I knew from the first time I picked up the mechanical pencil that this was what I wanted as a career. The trade school offered an 18-month course, with placement assistance upon

25

graduation. I checked out the instructors, their experience, and the reputation of the school, as well as placement records and the status of the students who had been placed. I tried to be as thorough as possible in my investigation. I made an effort to corroborate every statement I got from a company or an individual. I was about to make an important decision, and I didn't want it to backfire. My investigation turned up not one bad thing about this school. Fortunately everything people told me seemed to be true.

Meanwhile, my ongoing job at the hospital was just fine. I still enjoyed it; I just felt the department head didn't appreciate the amount of work I performed. And I knew from his statement to me that he had no confidence I would advance in the department.

I finished trade school with a B+ average, the second highest in a graduation class of more than 50 students. The placement assistant had set up two interviews for me, and both companies made me offers within two days. The position I took was as a basemap drafter with the city's gas and electric company. It was a second-shift job, giving me the chance to get acclimated before quitting my job at the hospital (where I had since been promoted to supervisor). This arrangement also doubled my income. My starting salary was equal to what I was making at the hospital after working there for more than six years. I worked both jobs for about six months.

With my career on the right track, I felt nothing could stop me now. I continued to work for the gas and electric company for the next five months. I worked hard and tried to learn as much as possible, all the while looking to the next step on the ladder.

I answered every ad for every job for which I felt qualified. At least 95 percent of the leads I followed up on came from the local newspaper. The other 5 percent came from friends and acquaintances. I soon discovered that my skills were not as impressive as I had thought. A lot of other people were looking for the same type of job. Some had more experience, some had less. I needed to recognize my true experience level. The main thing I had going for me was that I never lost confidence in my abilities. And I never lost my focus. There was always the big picture, and I never lost sight of it.

I sent out a minimum of 12 résumés per week. Rejection letters pointed out that I wasn't experienced enough or didn't have the correct schooling for the position. From each letter I learned something else about my résumé, and made the necessary changes. I

27

never lied, but I did learn what to enhance and what to leave out, and what the person reading it wished to see.

Each interview also taught me a lesson. I'd ask the interviewer what in my résumé made him wish to contact me. When I wasn't offered the position, I'd ask why not and what I'd done wrong in the interview. I asked what I should have done or how I should have answered. I took away something I could use each and every time I was interviewed. I worked hard to develop my skills for the interview process. I learned to anticipate the questions I'd be asked and what my answers would be. I learned to put the interviewer on the defensive and to be more comfortable in the interview than the interviewer. Five months may not seem like a long time to develop the skills I'm talking about, but when you are interviewing on an almost daily basis, believe me, you learn fast. Finally, all the hard work and time invested paid off. I was offered a job with a company that was doing upgrade work aboard Navy ships.

From each letter I learned something else about my résumé, and made the necessary changes. I never lied, but I did learn what to enhance and what to leave out, and what the person reading it wished to see.

I was faced with a decision that would affect my life and that of my fiancée. In accepting this position, I would be forced to take a major pay cut. The fact that we had just purchased our first home about two months earlier made the decision all the harder. I felt strongly about the situation, and she stood by me. I believed that the position would be better for me as far as advancement and experience than my present job with the gas and electric company. I wanted the most experience I could get as fast as I could get it.

This decision proved to be a wise one. The pay cut did hurt us for a while, but we made it through. My supervisor was to become one the most influential people in my career. He was willing to work with me to teach me what I wished to learn, and I showed him that I was willing to do whatever I had to, to learn as much as he was willing to teach me. He never held me back, never told me I was trying to learn too fast, never felt threatened by my enthusiasm to learn. I was lucky to find such a person to teach me, someone with whom I could also become good friends.

I worked hard to prove myself and my skills at this job, and things went well for the next six months. My progress was noticed by all in the office. My supervisor placed me

29

in charge of the design of the office's piping section. This meant I would be surpervising people who had been doing this type of work for four or five years—even though I had only been in the field for six months. You would expect problems to arise with this arrangement, but the staff had seen how hard I worked and the efforts I had made to prove myself. They understood that the corrections I requested were necessary. They knew the position I had been placed in wasn't over—or hadn't gone to—my head. My supervisory training from the hospital helped me make the transition to this new position. But all good things must come to an end. Three months later, the company lost the Navy contract and closed our office.

With this setback, I needed employment immediately. Some people think they should take only the job they are trained for and not something that helps pay the bills, but I disagree. Some people say they won't take a certain job because they feel it's beneath them. But every job has to be done. At this point in my life, the most important thing was to be able to generate some type of income. So I went back to what I knew best. I landed a job as a warehouse manager at a party rental company. It meant another pay cut, but it kept me bringing home a steady income. And

30

I had time to look for another job in the design field.

For the next nine months, I worked as a warehouse manager. I gave it my all, the only way I know how to work. I made the changes I thought would make the company run more efficiently. I arrived early and left late. Based on my performance, my boss could never have known that I was looking for another job. I asked for raises and got them.

All the while, I stayed in contact with my mentor, my supervisor from my last job. He never lost faith in me. He gave me design exercises to keep my skills sharp. He also suggested those companies to which he felt I should apply. As I said before, I was lucky to find such a supervisor and friend.

With all the résumés and word of mouth about me, it was just a matter of time before something came along. Finally, the call came. I got an interview for a position as a designer with a fire sprinkler company. How I got the interview was remarkable. Apparently, the interviewer had originally called in 12 people to interview. From those 12, he selected four he considered the best. By the time he was ready to offer the job to his first choice, the person had accepted another offer. Of the three remaining, one had an offer from another company, the other had moved, and the third

31

was no longer interested. I was only number 13 on his list, but I got the call. I had never believed in fate until that moment.

I took all the tests, filled out all the forms, and answered all the questions the interviewer posed. Four hours later, he offered me the position. Then came the catch: I would have to move to Tacoma, Washington, for six months of training at the company's facility. Since we had just bought a new home, this presented a problem, but I accepted the job anyway. Again, I had that strong feeling, and again, my fiancée supported my decision. Now we had to figure out if we both would go to Tacoma or if it would be easier for me to go alone. Because our house was only a year old, we weren't too fond of the idea of renting it out for six months. We decided I would go to Tacoma alone. Six months turned out not to be so long after all.

This company was a great place to work. The benefits were great, the pay was great, the people were great, and my supervisor became another mentor. I'm a person who tends to get bored unless there's a variety of things to keep me occupied. Recognizing this, my supervisor made sure it didn't happen. I also went to him for additional duties. All the work habits and experience I had gained at my other jobs—along with my own work ethic—now

32

propelled me into this new career. I applied myself to the job and did the best I could, never losing my thirst for knowledge, and never taking criticism as personal but only as a lesson to be learned. Although I had been through the six-month training course, I didn't assume that I had all the answers or that I knew it all. Most of the people in the office had vast experience in the field. The person with the least amount of experience, next to me, was my office mate, who had two years. I understood from the start that this field would take time to master. I understood that I needed to take time to learn this job to its fullest before trying to move up.

I still can't say if it was luck, fate, or my own hard work and dedication. I like to think that hard work and dedication to your job and company are the things that move you up the ladder of success. Two years and six months into this job, I was promoted to estimator in the service department. The district manager had fired the service manager and he brought in a new person to run the department. To my good fortune, it seemed that this new service manager was very high on in-house promotions. In an executive meeting, the question was asked, "Who would be the best person for the position of service estimator?" Apparently, my name was unanimously voiced. With this

33

promotion and the company's progressive policies, I felt this was a company from which I could retire. Everything was unfolding the way I had dreamed.

Ten years later, I have since moved on but have worked for some other terrific companies. Now I am a service manager for a branch office of the largest union fire sprinkler company in the United States. My family lives in a modest middle-class neighborhood. I am always looking to upgrade my position and increase my income. My work ethic has not changed one bit. I'm one of the first people in the office each day and one of the last to leave. It does help a great deal that I enjoy my work and that I like the people I work with as well as the company I work for.

This is the route I took in playing the Game. This is how a poor kid born in racially segregated Mississippi—raised by his grandmother and great-grandmother—ended up in the Pacific Northwest living a *Leave It to Beaver* lifestyle. Dreams do come true. My life now is what I dreamed it would be. It is the life I saw as the American dream. It is the life depicted on those television shows that so influenced me when I was young.

As I reflect back on those television shows, they depicted mainly a conservative, mainstream view of life: a father who works outside the home; a mother who maintains the household; a middle-class neighborhood with tree-lined streets; good, wholesome kids who for the most part obeyed their parents; individuality; dedication to family; living life to its fullest. These are the things I took away from those shows. And these are the things I felt I wanted for my future family. Put them together with my own thoughts and ideas, throw in the values and morals of my grandmother and great-grandmother, spice it up with different environments, shake well, and you get me.

I like to think I never lost my dreams, just maybe set them aside for a while to explore. If you always keep your dreams with you—if only in the back of your mind—you will no doubt work for them to come true, whether consciously or unconsciously. The key to a successful you is dreaming and being able to hold fast to those dreams.

Chapter Two

I think that kids today have a greater opportunity than I did. It's much more doable than it was 30 years ago. The limitations to someone being able to achieve something isn't as much racially or ethnically related as it is economically related. That's why I'm a proponent of making the economy grow as healthy and as strong as we possibly can.

—Herman Cain, CEO, Godfather's Pizza

36

The Playing Field:
The Workplace

Fight stereotypes in the workplace.

It's wrong that the white man perceives
the black man in certain ways, but he does.
The only way to change his view of us is to
do the job as well as the white man.

37

I magine that you own a business and have people like yourself working there. Consider this honestly: Would you be happy with the job you perform? How would you feel if the business you owned was being held back because some employees felt it wasn't their job to help that business succeed? How would you feel if they actually resented the fact that the business was a success? Would you want them working for you?

If you aren't working to help a business, then you may as well not be there. The owner didn't start his business so that you would have a job. He also doesn't hire people off the street because they need a job. He hires the people he thinks will help his business prosper.

The main purpose of any business is to provide profits to its owners and stockholders. If you expect to receive any rewards from the work you perform, you must invest yourself in

39

your job. The average worker may always be steady, but average work is all he can produce. He can keep his job, but when it comes to that promotion, he comes up a little short. As a black man in the workplace, you must always be above average, and there is no reason why you can't be.

When you're the only black man in a workplace, you will always be on display. You must always be on your toes. You must keep your wits about you. You must keep your focus. Success for you doesn't make you any less black or any more white. It makes you smart and independent, able to do as you wish, able to take care of your family. The brothers on the corner may give you all the grief they can muster, but until they're able to pay you for what you do, their talk is just that, talk. Their inability to handle your success is their problem, not yours. For you to screw up your job and jeopardize the livelihood of your family just to look good in their eyes would be plain stupid.

When I think of the workplace, a fear that comes to mind is the total lack of effort put forth by the black man. I can remember tip-offs on how to sleep in the rest room, where to hide out, how to look busy when you're doing nothing, how to take the defensive when you're attacked for not doing your job, and how to use the race issue at every opportunity to prove you are being singled out. These words may be harsh, and may put you on the defensive, but they are some of my firsthand, real-life experiences.

This is what I heard and saw as I entered the Game at the bottom rung of the ladder. Although I knew these things were wrong, I did fall prey to peer pressure. Deep in the back of my mind, I knew I wasn't doing right by my employer. It took a while to overcome the peer pressure, but I finally did, and things were different from then on. As I began to move up into positions with more income and responsibility, I watched as my black coworkers stayed in their same old jobs. I was accused of "selling out the race to the white man to get the token job." How could my taking a job that I had desired be considered a sellout to my entire race? Just because it didn't fit their idea of working? I didn't get it.

I did, however, notice that I had been at my job for a lot less time than most of the blacks there, and I advanced over them. The fact that I showed I had the same initiative and drive as the white man somehow made me a sellout to my race. Could that be right? I don't think so. After all, I was there to do a job, not to make a stand with my brothers about race. But still I was called the Uncle Tom, the sell-out, the token.

41

Why did the other blacks resent the fact that I was promoted and they weren't? They had to have noticed that there was a difference between my work ethic and theirs. They had to have noticed that each day I came to work long before them, that I worked a little harder than they did, that I asked for more responsibility than they did, that I wasn't at their screw-off places, that my work was somehow completed and theirs wasn't. These facts had to be on their minds as their resentment for me grew. I decided I wasn't about to give up the job I needed just because a few of my people felt I had sold out. The resentment they felt for me was something I would have to live with, and I adjusted my mind to deal with it.

The owner doesn't hire people off the street because they need a job. He hires the people he thinks will help his business prosper.

Still I wondered, Why had I become the target of their resentment? My conclusion: They resented me because I took away their easy way of working. It was no longer feasible not to expect more from them. I proved that blacks could have work ethics and could be more than they were. I forced them to work in order to get somewhere. No longer could they hide behind the charge that the white man was holding them down. No longer could they

42

be angry at the white man because things weren't going their way. As a black man on his way up, I made it apparent that the only reason they weren't getting anywhere was their own fault. I took away the excuse that the work world wasn't fair to blacks. This is why they resented me. It took me a while to figure these things out. Once I did, it didn't make it any easier to handle their resentment, but it did help me deal with the situation better.

You will face racism in the workplace, but exemplary work and good performance can overcome that. It takes a lot out of a person to have to continually put up with negative attitudes—at work and at home. But if we can make it through the job each day, then we will also be able to handle the negativity we face. I know I certainly felt better at the end of the week as I passed the brothers on the corner to go to the bank, and all they could do was stand and watch and make comments. This feeling helped keep me going. My reward was the paycheck at the end of the week for a job well done. My promotions through the ranks were my return for hard work and dedication to the company. These rewards are tangible. You put effort in, and you receive something in return.

> **You will face racism in the workplace, but exemplary work and good performance can overcome that.**

43

Another key to a rewarding career or job is enjoying the work you do to the point that the job becomes easy. I heard my great-grandmother once tell a friend who was feeling down in the dumps about her job, "If you don't enjoy the job you do, it's just work." I've remembered that all my life and always searched for a job I enjoyed doing. (Thanks, Great-grandmama.)

Success doesn't make you any less black or any more white. It makes you smart and independent, able to do as you wish, able to take care of your family.

You should always make the effort to excel in the job you are performing. Each time you perform a step in the process of doing your job, look for a better way to do it. You will often find that the effort you put into improving your job will be directly related to the income you receive.

You may well be in a job that does not suit you or that you are not happy doing. You must still perform the job to the best of your ability until you are able to change the situation; at least when you do leave that job, you will have a decent recommendation from the company. As long as they sign your paychecks, you owe them your best.

Never burn your bridges. Just because you may be leaving to take another position

44

doesn't mean you have to leave on bad terms. I can think of only one former company where I couldn't reapply. At some, I could walk in the door today, and the owner or manager would remember me and my work there. Leave a company with the idea that you did your best, and that you are moving on to bigger and better things. No business manager would find fault in a person trying to better himself.

The White Man's Perception of Blacks

For many black men, time in the workplace is like being on foreign soil. They are not at ease with coworkers or customers. Every hour of every workday, they are on the lookout for evidence of discrimination, or are looking for some way to "get one over" on the company. Now, this doesn't represent the attitude of every black man in the workplace, but keep in mind that this is the perception the white man has of the black man. It is a heavy burden to overcome, but overcome it we can!

If we are to be judged as a group and stereotyped that way, then we must go to the root—others' perception of the black race— and change it. I don't say these things about the white man to charge him with negativism; I say them to make you as a black man aware of them. Take all the things I'm saying about

45

the white man and use them as they are intended, to educate you to the ways in the white man's work world. We need his perception of us to be as positive as possible.

Most black people have the attitude that the company they work for owes them something. Nobody owes anyone—black or white—a career. You must prove that you are able to perform the job, and that you deserve the chance to do more. Not to live up to your full potential while performing a job will only hurt you, whereas the company will most likely survive.

Value Systems and Work Ethics

The thoughts and ideas in this guide are the rules by which I live. Everyone has to have such rules; your values may differ from others', but you must have something as your compass. The lack of values and the inability of parents to communicate to their children the basics for leading a good and decent life are among the main reasons for the black community's current dilemma in this country. We as a society must have certain values that we pass on to our children in order for our society to survive. The black community is deteriorating at a rapid pace due to this lack of values and the loss of the family unit. Black people can blame this deterioration on whomever they wish, but until we take the

46

blame and make the change, our downfall in this white man's world will continue.

Many blacks arrive at a company with a grudge and a chip on their shoulder. They are looking for slights and unfairness. Because most blacks are isolated from mainstream white society, they have no idea how to interact with people outside their race. And when they try to be a part of the crowd at the workplace, they find that the expected common ground and their ideas of fun and leisure are totally different from the other people's.

It is very hard to perform your job while trying to be someone you're not. This is one of the leading causes of stress. You must feel comfortable in your workplace and with the people around you. Don't feel like you have to be best friends, or that you have to agree with them all the time, but you should make an attempt to get to know them and enjoy them. After all, you do have one big thing in common—you're all in the same working world.

Some blacks may say to themselves, "Let them get to know things about me and my race." That would be my suggestion also if we were in charge, if we had the power, if we created most of the jobs, if we held the majority of the wealth in this country. But we don't. We are the ones who must change in order to get what we deserve. I know you have all heard the

47

statement IT'S A MAN'S WORLD. Well, take that one step further: IT'S A WHITE MAN'S WORLD.

If you are not willing to accept certain things in life as absolutes and deal with them from the point of view that you are not the one who makes the rules but the one who follows the rules, you may as well pack your bags and move to some deserted island. It's an absolute that for most of your life, you will work for the white man. It's an absolute that the rules will be made by the white man and followed or broken by the black man. It's an absolute that without a good education, you will go nowhere in the workplace. How you relate to these absolutes will condition your life in the work world. These factors will define your position and where you go in this white man's world.

You must be sure to develop your work ethics no matter what job you have. These ethics will define your place in the work world. They will earn you the respect of your peers. The work ethics you develop while getting started in the Game will be invaluable to you once you find your niche.

The black man must realize that he will have no well-defined role in the Game, because relatively few of us have embarked upon the road to success in the corporate world. We have few precedents to follow. This is why the work

48

ethics you develop for yourself are so important. You must put your best foot forward at all times. When you make it, you must always be ready to show and tell the younger brothers of the life you've achieved and how you've achieved it. Don't try to be a hero. Just tell them what worked and what didn't. This is where the next generation will get their success stories and their role models, and you will get your immortality.

You must understand things from the white man's point of view. The white man wonders if the black man has the same interests as he does. And if not, why not? He fears all the things he has heard and read about the black man, no matter how wrong they may be. It is up to us to put his mind at ease, to make him understand that we are not monsters but simply people with a different heritage. It is our job to try to make the white man feel at ease around us and the best opportunity to do that is in the workplace. We can make him understand that our hopes and dreams are fundamentally the same as his, that we wish to excel in our careers and to provide for our families as he does.

49

The white man has the power. In order for us to share in that power, we must change our ways. Although the white man invented the Game, there is no reason why we can't play it as well as he does. We must show the white man that our work ethics are like his. He must feel assured that we have prepared for the job as hard as he has and that we are as committed to it. These are some of the things we have to relay to the white man through our actions in the workplace.

It's only natural that the white man has had the same prejudices pushed upon him about us as we have had about him. There are people in our generation who had their first experience with a person of another race in college, in the service, or in the workplace. Despite years of being told how bad the other race was, most people's first encounter is positive. They find that most of the rhetoric about the other race was greatly exaggerated. They find that each race is unique, but we all want the same thing in our careers and for our families. Because of the many preconceptions about blacks, the black man must show a more consistently positive lifestyle so those preconceptions begin to change.

Our best chance to save the next generation from the life we're suffering through is

I proved that blacks could have work ethics. No longer could they hide behind the charge that the white man was holding them down. As a black man on his way up, I took away the excuse that the work world wasn't fair to blacks. This is why they resented me.

by defining our place in the work world. It is up to us not only to leave the trail of bread crumbs for the younger brothers to follow, but to ensure that the brothers are able to find them. And once they do, we must ensure that they can understand the message.

We must pass on to the younger brothers the lessons that our experiences have taught us. Unfortunately, most of us try to teach the younger brothers without having learned the lessons ourselves. How do you teach your kids work ethics and wholesome living when you haven't tried them yourself? This was my problem with the brothers on the corner telling me how to live my life.

I had to avoid falling into the same trap of trying to tell the younger brothers how to live their lives while I lived mine differently. I realized that the only way to teach was by example. And although my life isn't perfect, I try to live it consistently with the advice I give to my son. It would be great if this advice were given to all the younger brothers. It would be wonderful if we went out to the schools and to the boys' and girls' clubs to speak to kids with a different message than the old white man blame game. It would be the best thing for our race if the black youth of today hear from good role models that the plight of the black man is not just the fault of the white man, but mainly of his own doing.

51

Success

Failures are a part of life. Ask any successful businessman how many times he tried before he made it. I'm sure that most have tried more than once. Without ever taking a risk, without wishing to take charge of one's life, being afraid of failure is like being afraid of success. For without failure, there would be no measurement of success.

True success is a personal thing. Success to one person is not necessarily success to another. So you should never base your idea of success on how others judge it. Your idea of success and how to achieve it has to come from within you. You must make a commitment to that success and have the motivation to achieve it. You must prepare for it and be ready to travel the long, hard road to it. You must be prepared for life's failures and disappointments along the way. You must be ready to accept each failure, reboot your motivation, and carry on.

As a race, our success will come from our people. Our biggest challenge will be to change the attitudes of other groups about who a black man is. We have to demonstrate that we are willing to work hard and take care of our families. We must show our kids the right roads to follow. We must be willing to help the white man understand that our life is no different from his;

52

we deal with the same problems he does and have the same concerns he has.

As I write these words, they bring back memories of my past. They remind me of the hard work it took to get to where I am today. All the work and dedication I put in at the beginning is now paying off. I have a job I love. I'm able to choose when and where I wish to work, and I dictate the salary I am paid. My life mirrors what I grew up thinking the American dream would be.

The Game has been tough, but it hasn't been unfair. My preparation took longer than the conventional route, but I overcame that. The jobs I've had over the years have been good and bad, but only briefly did I lose my motivation to win at the Game.

Enabling your children to watch you enjoy winning the Game will give them the same desire to win it. We must keep the children motivated to keep our race strong. That is our supreme legacy. Let's maintain that our lives will be the main teaching tool for our children.

One of the main things to remember about the workplace is this: It is the job of the black man to change how others perceive him. The change in the perception of the black man will no doubt benefit the black race. Everything is in place for us to succeed in this country; we must take advantage of it. All the opportunity in the world is right here in front of us.

53

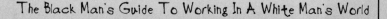

As a boy, my grandfather worked in a Jewish bakery in Springfield, Missouri, and spoke fluent Yiddish. Throughout Kansas and Missouri he was extremely successful at building bridges because he understood both cultures and he understood his role in them. His role was to build bridges to bring people together. As a Congressman that would be my role as well.

—Colorado congressional candidate Joe Rogers

The Players:
Us and Them

Sharpen your communication skills.

Speak the language of those ahead in the
Game, and you'll catch up quickly.

55

While growing up in Mississippi I remember going with my grandmother to her job as a maid in the house of a white doctor and his wife. She did the cooking, cleaning, laundry, shopping, and gardening. But my reason for tagging along was not to see the things she did for the white man, but to play with the doctor's grandkids. This was my first real experience with white kids. Before, they were only people on TV. These kids did seem like the TV characters; they sounded like Beaver and they wanted to play the same games. They were totally different from my friends at home.

One big difference I noticed right away was their neighborhood. Where I lived, a multitude of fences separated the yards, as if to say THIS IS MINE AND THAT IS YOURS. The white kids' neighborhood, on the other hand, had less fences and more space. It was like one very

57

large yard for the kids to play in. It seemed that all of the property belonged to the neighborhood and not just to one person. We played in all the yards, and no one chased us out. The kids whose backyards we ran through would come out and play with us as if they knew us real well. And these white kids I played with had no intention of doing anything that would upset the neighborhood. They never suggested we do anything that we knew was wrong or would get us into trouble. This was my idea of how playtime should be.

The best thing I got from that experience was that when I was around those kids, I felt no different from them. This was where I wanted to be. Not because they were white, but because this was the way I had pictured life to be.

But when the day was over, I had to return to the reality of my neighborhood until the next time.

Returning to my neighborhood was very difficult. Eager to tell my friends how I had spent my day, I discovered that it was not something they wished to hear. I couldn't understand why they weren't interested in my newfound friends or the games we played, in something they didn't know. They gave me the cold shoulder, saying, "Here comes little Mr. Oreo." What was the difference between them and me? Why was I able to play and have fun with kids they considered to be so different? Eventually, I ended up playing the games they wanted and doing the things I was used to doing.

But I always thought of the differences between the two groups: how interested the white kids were in my life back home with my black friends and how uninterested my black friends were in the lives of those white kids. I also noticed the differences in the grown-ups. In my neighborhood, the grown-ups naturally made comments about the white man and his kids, and these comments were always said so the kids could hear. But the white grown-ups never commented about what they thought was wrong with the black man. Perhaps it just didn't come out while I was around, though you would think that the kids would express some of the feelings their parents had about blacks. I cannot remember anything said to me or about blacks that was derogatory.

The childhood of the typical black man is not the way it is portrayed on television programs. We don't get shipped off to some rich uncle in Bel-Air and most of the parents who are together are not lawyers and doctors. Most of us grow up in poverty or close to it. This is where the loss of self-esteem occurs. Black kids witness their mother, or sometimes

59

both parents, working hard, barely earning enough to get by and complaining about it.

Perhaps it is only natural that black kids then wonder why they should work hard at school to prepare for a life of barely getting by. What the kids don't realize (and their parents don't fess up about) is that the parents aren't educated. We need to be able to be truthful with our kids about the reasons we do not receive what we are worth or what we perceive we are worth. It is not the white man's fault, it is not the government's fault, it is our own fault. It is the fault of parents who choose not to explain why they have dead-end jobs, why they didn't provide themselves with the proper education and training so they could do better. We must stop giving the impression that the blame lies with someone else. We must at some point break this chain of thought, or it will destroy our race. The kids need to know the correct way to play the Game. And the only way they will learn is if the present generation teaches them. We are the ones who can set the stage for our youth. We must start thinking about our kids.

In my experience, white kids are taught early on that education is needed to succeed. Even if a white family is poor and the parents weren't able to attend college or are in low-paying jobs, the idea of education is stressed in the household. The white man may complain about his life, but he also lets his kids know it is his fault and no one else's, and he generally has the well-being of his kids in mind. He thinks ahead, his focus being on the future and his kids. The white man passes the correct messages on to his kids, and his spirit lives through them. This is his immortality. As long as his kids remember his examples and lessons, his race will thrive.

Black people need to adopt some of the white man's ideas for our kids to win at the Game. And we don't have to lose our "black" culture to be able to succeed in the white man's world. The world, as we know it in the United States, does and will probably always belong to the white man. We, as the black race, must learn to live with this and adapt ourselves to get by in his world. Do we really think the white man in America will give up to us his power, his wealth, and his prestige simply because of the guilt we assume he has over the treatment of our forefathers by his forefathers? Not a chance. The white man will never give up his position, just as the black man—if he were to control life in America—would not give up his. All other

> The white man will never give up his position, just as the black man—if he were to control life in America—would not give up his.

61

races in this country must understand this and live their lives accordingly.

As long as whites are doing the giving, you can believe that they will give you no more than you need to merely help yourself out of the rut. They will give you just enough to keep you happy and dependent upon them for more, but never enough to put you on the same plane, because that would constitute a transfer of power. The transfer of power from the white race to the black race will never happen unless the black race makes it happen by changing the way they live. The white man will never give up the power he has just for the sake of bringing the races together. He would never willingly lose his power base.

Many national black leaders think that because of the white man's good intentions, things will get better for us. These leaders have become confused by the easy life they receive from the system, while things remain the same for lower-class blacks. Why? Because we keep believing the talk and do nothing to help ourselves. This is the power the white man has over us, and it is a power we willingly give him. We believe that he will give us something for free which will make us productive members of society. But instead we continue to live in poverty and complain about the things others have that we don't.

It is amazing how Japan has become such a leading global power since the end of World War II. It is because they took a page from the white man's book and then developed their own system—what they considered was best suited to their way of life. What makes the Japanese people unique still exists. They are no less Japanese because of the ideas they use. If anything, they are better off, economically and culturally.

The black race must look at the Japanese and how they adapted the changes as a conscious effort by the entire country and its people. They started with the post–World War II generation, and trained the next generation to adapt. That generation, in turn, taught their children. Within two generations, the change has taken hold and has become the norm.

This shows that the change must be made by the entire race, that it can't be done by a few to pave the way for the rest. The present generation has the burden to make the change work. If it isn't willing to change, the plan is doomed from the start.

If, using the white man's ideas, the black race can attain half the success of the Japanese, we will be ten times better off for it. The Japanese did it by instilling a value system, training their present generation and

63

educating the next generation. The Asians, even more than the white man, impress on their kids the rewards of education.

Two people go in for an interview: one is black, one is Asian. They're applying to a Fortune 500 company, headed by white men. Who's more likely to get the job? The Asian. Why?

Number one: stereotyping. Both the black man and the Asian have been stereotyped—but the black man will be perceived as lazy, undereducated, and looking for a free ride under the guise of affirmative action, whereas the Asian will be perceived as hardworking, well educated, and dedicated. The white man will tend to believe that any other race will produce a better worker than the black race will.

Number two: the interview itself. The white man is apt to choose the person who most resembles himself. This involves language, demeanor, and value system, as perceived by the white man.

How can we overcome this? The white man feels pressure to hire the black man because he will stand out more prominently in the workplace than other races; affirmative action is usually affiliated with blacks. Take advantage of this, and prepare yourself for the interview. Think of possible questions, and rehearse your answers. Know something about the company.

Know why you want to work there. Know how you want to advance in the company. These are things that any potential employer expects to hear from a job applicant.

The national black leaders are so far removed from the lifestyle of the common black man. Instead of offering us more programs to "help" us, let them show us how to start playing the Game in the white man's world. They themselves have been playing it long enough. They know all the tricks of the trade.

> The national black leaders are so far removed from the lifestyle of the common black man. Instead of offering us more programs to "help" us, let them show us how to start playing the Game in the white man's world.

We need to lobby the government as a group of educated black people. We need employers and the government to be confident that we are just as good at doing a job as anyone else in this great country. We don't need programs to build animosity between the races. Our leaders and the power brokers in Washington must understand that the only thing we need is a fair chance.

The big difference between the races is the white man has the power. And the people without the power will always feel that they are receiving the short end of the stick. Don't read this as a protest against the white man or

65

as praise for him. The white man is only doing what comes naturally: protecting his own. No other race would do differently.

Other non-white races have figured it out, and most have not been here as long as the black race. They understand that they must work hard to achieve their dreams. They join together and work as a race for what they want. But most important, they never forget those who will follow after them—the children. They pave the way for them, to make their path easier. Other races take the handouts given by the white man and use them to get ahead. The black race just keeps taking the handouts.

Probably the major difference between the white man and the black man is that the white man is taught from the beginning, by his parents' example, that education and hard work are the route to success. The black man is usually left to his own devices, from early childhood on, to learn this for himself—if at all. This results from the lack of the family unit, the lack of positive parenting, the lack of a wholesome environment. All you need to do is take a walk through any U.S. city mall, or go to any family restaurant or activity center and count the number of white families and the number of black families. I'll bet you dollars to doughnuts there will be more white families than black families. By families, I mean in the traditional manner of speaking: a mother, a father, and kids.

Children in black families are usually being raised by the mother, whether the father is in the home or not. The father is usually too consumed with his status in the eyes of the brothers on the corner to pay much attention to his own children. He cares more about what these brothers say about him than about the well-being of his family. It's like a blow to his manhood to be involved with his children. Being perceived as participating in family activities somehow makes him less of a man. He has to be free to present himself as the head of the household without really being there. His family is not to be cherished and taken care of; it's only there to prove to the community that he is a man.

The white man, on the other hand, is taught to cherish his family, to provide them with his love and support, which will be returned to him a hundredfold. He is taught that the family unit is the core of life. The white man who provides for his family is the man who has status in his community. He doesn't have to prove his manhood to anyone. The white man is taught that the care of the children is the job of both parents, and being the head of the household is not as important as being its provider.

67

If you want to change the human condition for the better, you cannot sit on the sidelines. We have a brilliant opportunity, the intellectual capital and the moral endurance to change anything in our path that's a negative. Open your date books, checkbooks and Bibles—the date books to donate your time, the checkbooks to spend your resources, and the Bible as your moral compass.

—J. Kenneth Blackwell

Don't get the wrong idea. I'm not saying that the white man has a lock on how life should be, but I am saying that he has a better idea about life as it relates to the family unit than the black man does. This is not to say that white families are problem free, because they're not. There is abuse in white families. There are the good-for-nothing fathers and the single mothers who raise kids alone. There is welfare fraud. But it seems these are the only examples blacks take from whites.

The black man, for the most part, was and still is not raised with the family unit in place. And even if he were, the majority of people in his neighborhood probably weren't. It's not the norm. All black families seem to have the same problems and complaints, which mostly have to do with the lack of money. This comes from the parents' insufficient education and lack of motivation. They become complacent with government handouts.

Another big factor that contributes to the hard times of the black family is the kids' lack of restraint regarding sexual activities. Our kids must be taught that they are likely to suffer damaging consequences if they pursue the lifestyle our liberal society has sanctioned. Our race will stay on the same downhill course if we don't teach our kids not to have kids until they are mentally, emotionally, and financially prepared.

There may be just as many young white girls having babies as young black girls, but we shouldn't concern ourselves with the shortcomings of the white race. This is one of the black race's problems: We can never use the negatives of another race to get to the positives of our own. If we could try to learn from the positive attributes of other races, we could change our race. To be a strong black race, we must strive to be better.

Why does the white man have such a different outlook on life than the black man? It seems to relate to the teaching of morals, which are not taught by sitting your kids down and explaining them. They are not taught simply by reading a book. They are taught by the example of your life. Because white kids are shown a different lifestyle, they have a better

69

start on life. They have a greater desire to succeed, a greater commitment to family, and greater pride in their jobs and their race. These are the morals we, the present generation, need to learn. These are the morals the kids need to be taught to make their lives better. Seems pretty simple to me.

Let's give it a try. Our present way of life certainly isn't working. We greet each other with "Hello, Brother," but it's just a hollow greeting. We say we have pride in our race, but the first chance we get to hurt one of our own, we do. We say we wish to succeed, but do nothing to help that dream along. We say that family is the core of the race, but we are never there to help the family once it's created. What we say we want and what we try to accomplish are two very different things.

We need the humility to accept and apply what works in white America without feeling like we're sacrificing some sacred black culture.

We show no pride in family, career, or race. We have lost the morals that taught us how to get through life. We have lost the desire to be civil to one another. We have lost sight of the difference between right and wrong. We have lost the things that separate us from the animals. Are we any better than animals when we go out in gangs seeking people and things to destroy? At least animals kill out of instinct and the desire for survival; we kill out of lack of morals and respect for our race and others.

Gangs, drug abuse, single mothers, the increasing high school dropout rate, welfare fraud, addiction, unemployment, teenage pregnancy, violence in our schools and streets—these are not unique to the black race, but we are the only race that seems to hold them dear. These problems are a gauge of the black race. We can easily measure our progress by them. Is our race in trouble? Do we need help from the white man? Yes, we are in trouble, but we don't need the white man's help. We need the help of our own communities, our own leaders, our own people, our own parents. We need to change how we live. We need the humility to accept and apply what works in white America without feeling like we're sacrificing some sacred black culture.

Webster's Dictionary defines culture as "the integrated pattern of human knowledge, belief, and behavior that depends upon man's capacity for learning and transmitting knowledge to succeeding generations: the customary beliefs, social forms, and material traits of a racial, religious, or social group." Have we, as the definition states, passed on to succeeding generations anything other than the

71

American culture? I know we talk a lot about the black culture, but do we really know what it is? Is there such a thing as black culture apart from American culture? Maybe there is for those born and raised in Africa, but I think not for blacks born and raised in America.

For us to have any chance of success in this country, our country, we need to evaluate our cultural traits. Are they more American or African or something else entirely? I think we will find them to be more American, and if this is so, then we need to take hold of the culture we live in and make it work for us.

The white man doesn't experience many of the same problems the black man does because the white man takes greater responsibility for himself and his own. When he finds himself in need, he doesn't look to the government for a handout, but to friends and family members who are more than willing to help—at least the first time. To see any of his own down on their luck and not lend a helping hand is against his interests. He is also generally able to provide the help needed. The government is only the white man's last resort. Government has its purpose, but it's not to help every Tom, Dick, and Harry off the street that refuses to help himself. The handouts we receive from the white man are the very things that allow him to have so

72

much control over us. Never turn down the things the white man gives, just never stop striving for more on your own. And always be wary. There will usually be a price to pay down the road.

Remember, it is the job of the white man to try to wield power over someone—as it is our job to make sure it isn't the black race. With the education and motivation we get as kids, we should be able to overcome anything the white man throws in our path. Let's make ourselves better and not wait for the white man to give us his hold-down handouts.

The handouts we receive from the white man are the very things that allow him to have so much control over us.

Here's a joke: WHAT SCARES A WHITE MAN MORE THAN A BLACK MAN WITH A GUN? A BLACK MAN WITH AN EDUCATION. The white man may have to oppress someone, but it doesn't have to be us. He oppresses us because we allow it to happen. We don't educate ourselves, we don't participate in the Game to the extent we should, we don't learn the ways of the white man and use them to our advantage.

Another noticeable difference between "us" and "them" is the amount of respect white kids have for their parents and their parents' wishes and commands. Things they are told not to do, they don't do.

73

I observed as a child that white parents took time to explain things their kids didn't understand. And the kids listened. You could see in their eyes that they actually cared about what their parents were saying. I don't remember seeing such attentiveness in the eyes of my black friends.

With some conscious change on our part, we can make "them" think of "us" as not so different.

I suppose I was lucky to have a chance to see that this other life was for real. I was also fortunate because the school I attended was a private Catholic school that my mom, my uncle, my aunt, my cousins all attended in their day. The kids of black professionals went to school there, too, and this gave me another perspective. These kids lived as the white people on television, but they were black. Their lives were very different from mine and those of my neighborhood friends. Seeing that blacks could live the same life as whites and be happy made all the difference in my life. Had I believed the stories I heard from the fellows on the corners, I would have followed the same path as them and my black peers. But wanting more from life than what I saw in my neighborhood kept me on the higher road. My great-grandmother's foresight and determination to provide me with a fine education set me on that road.

74

I am so grateful that my grandmother took me to work with her and that I got to play and mix with the white kids. I don't know if she planned it that way, but it worked. Observing different lifestyles and getting a good educational and moral base thanks to my family has given me the tools to make my life the best it can be. This is what I wish to pass on to my son. Is this too much to ask for the entire black race? I don't think so.

Change the perception the white man has of the black race and you will change his treatment of you. If the white man feels you are more like him in education, career, and dedication to family, he will tend to treat you more as an equal. This doesn't mean he will welcome you into his fold with open arms, but it does mean he'll give you a fair shake. If nothing else, he will judge you on your ability and not on the color of your skin. When you let him know that you expect all that government says you should have under some affirmative action program, it is you who makes sure the white man notices your skin color. The white man greatly resents this attitude, as well he should. Instead, we should be ready and willing to prove we are up to the challenges of the job being offered.

I'm going to share with you the secret of achieving the American dream: EDUCATION!

75

That's it. That's the start of it all. Provide yourself with a good education and it will give you the tools to live the dream. This is the secret I learned from all my dealings with the white man.

There is no doubt in my mind that there will always be an "us" and "them." But with some conscious change on our part, we can make "them" think of "us" as not so different. Think about it. Work on it.

Major Differences Between "Us" and "Them"

The major differences between the white man and the black man, other than skin color, are motivation, economic status, and lifestyle. Let us look more closely at each.

Motivation

The white man is seldom satisfied with where he is. He is always motivated to strive for more. This is the motivation the black man lacks. Despite not being satisfied with his situation, the black man does little about it. He talks about how unhappy he is and blames others for not having what he thinks he deserves. He relies on the government to dictate how he should be treated instead of taking responsibility and standing up for himself. The driving force behind taking responsibility is motivation.

76

Economic Status

This refers to how society pigeonholes us by class. Countless studies have shown that parents' economic status has little to do with where kids end up on the social ladder. Their parents' economic status will of course afford kids access to better educational institutions, and possibly open some doors for them. But to assume that you are fundamentally disadvantaged because your parents don't have as elevated an economic status as others is plain stupid. You may have to work harder, but you can accomplish the same things. Here again, you need motivation.

Lifestyle

If America is the giant melting pot it's said to be, then we're all just Americans with different lifestyles. The black man needs to bring what's positive about his lifestyle into the mainstream and say THIS IS US, THIS IS WHAT WE ARE ABOUT. The lifestyle of the black man shouldn't be strange, just different.

77

The unemployment rate for blacks is 2.5 times the rate for whites. Our per-capita income is not even 2/3 of the income for whites; and blacks...are 3 times more likely to have income below the poverty level than whites. It has begun to seem that blacks, particularly black men, who lack at least two college degrees, are not hired in positions above the menial.

—Professor Derrick Bell

78

The Warm-Up: Preparation

Educate yourself.

If you don't, you will go from one low-paying
"No Experience Necessary" job to another.
If you do, you will have more to offer, get a
better job, and gain more control of your
income.

To prepare for the Game, you must first realize your desire to be in it and to be successful at it. The desire to win is a must. To play the Game and be involved is good, but to play with the hunger to win is great.

I grew up attending a parochial school. My wife and I agree that in order to give our son the same good base to build his learning skills, he will attend the best school we can find for as long as we can afford it. We truly believe this is the best way to get him started on the road to a good education. I am convinced of the benefit of this start because it's how I started.

Not everyone can attend private schools, which is why public schools must be improved to match the level of private schools. Just because a child attends a private school doesn't make him a better student. Public schools do

81

have their good points, too. Children still have to apply themselves to the lessons being taught. They still need to study and work hard to achieve good grades.

We hear that a great number of the kids graduating from public high schools aren't ready to enter college. They lack the basic skills to develop into work-world careers. Many have no desire to continue their education beyond high school. They have no need to believe that there is a better life for them. We must remove these thoughts from their minds.

Preparation entails a lot more than acquiring book sense. It's having common sense.

It is difficult to prepare for the Game, but millions of people have completed the preparation and become successful. It's not impossible, but it does take a lot of effort. There will no doubt be various obstacles to overcome: the lure of easy drug money, the pressure to join gangs, the constant banter of the older brothers on the corner telling how they can't get ahead because the white man has a conspiracy to keep them down, the peer pressure to be one of the crowd and not a nerd or bookworm, the fear of not making it through the neighborhood alive. Your desire to overcome these things must be strong. You must be strong. You must stay focused on your long-term dreams.

You may feel that there is little support for you, and at times you may feel as if you are all alone. But many others are involved in the same struggle. You may not see them or know them, but they're there.

Preparation entails a lot more than acquiring book sense. It's having common sense. It's recognizing help and taking advantage of what is available to provide you with the tools you need to make your life the best possible. It's being prepared for the unexpected. It's listening to your elders and believing they have some idea of what they speak. Preparation is about dreaming and then living your life in a way that enables you to achieve those dreams. It's about imagining what can happen in the future. It's about learning. It's about being all you can be. It's about taking control of your life.

As parents, we need to take our kids by the hand and lead them to the fork in the road. Give them the first choice of which road to take. As they start down that road, we need to stay by them and watch them along the way. And if we have done our jobs, the kids will take the right roads and stay on the straight and narrow. We can only lead them to the roads. We can't tell them which roads to take.

We can't attempt to relive our lives through them. We can't attempt to use them to right the mistakes we made growing up. But we can make their lives a little easier by telling them about what happened to us. Parents should show by example how best to achieve life's goals.

Too often, parents wish to teach their kids through their words more than through their actions. We can't do one thing and tell our kids it's OK for us and not for them. We have to walk our talk, or the message will never get through. We must understand that kids pick role models and heroes for various reasons. You may be a role model to your child and not realize it, so you must live your life as if you were a role model. We have to make our lives a lesson for the kids we encounter. If we lose another generation to crime and drugs, our America may be gone forever.

We all need to see that there is something more. This will enable the kids to take leadership of the country and make our twilight years tolerable. I am in the process of working hard now to support my son, and when I am no longer able to do so, I expect him to work hard to support me. I don't expect my son to relegate my wife and me to government programs for our care in our declining years. I hope that we raise him in a way that shows him how to correctly lead his life. I hope that he realizes his role in life from the examples we have provided. Isn't this how societies have functioned for thousands of years?

Part of the preparation involves learning what makes a person relevant to society. These are the morals and values that should be taught by parents. I don't think it's the job of schools to teach my kid morals—in a general sense, maybe, but not to the point of what he or she should believe in or stand for. We are on the verge of raising morally bankrupt kids. They need to receive positive, feel-good messages from somewhere, and that somewhere is from the home.

You may find that a school education doesn't come as easily for you as for others. Some people will breeze through subjects you are having problems with, but don't let that discourage you, because everyone learns differently. Some grasp concepts faster than others. There will be some subjects and assignments that you think will never be of use to you, but you are wrong. I used to think the same thing but have since realized that everything taught in school is for a reason. Everything you study in school will become important at some time in your life. From the perspective of preparing for the Game there are certain subjects that will require more of your attention. These subjects will become evident as you decide the direction you wish your career to take.

85

I see my time in school like this: Grammar school was a place to acquire the fundamentals of how to learn; junior high school was the place to apply those fundamentals and learn more difficult aspects of the courses; and high school was the place to test these fundamentals and pursue even more difficult courses. High school was the place where I tried to find my niche, and it gave me some direction toward my career. Some things will come easy and some will be more difficult, but this lets you know what subjects you need to work on more than others.

Part of the preparation involves learning what makes a person relevant to society.

College is the place to take all the fundamentals and lessons you have learned since grammar school and apply them as best you can to the real-work lessons taught there. But college is not the last place to learn in your preparation for the Game. Learning will always go on, even when you consider yourself a success at the Game.

There is talk of changing all the unemployment offices into training and retraining centers. Retraining centers are fine. To help retrain someone with legitimate marketable skills and real-world work experience for another field is totally acceptable. Then it would be up to the individual to accept responsibility for his or her own education.

All Americans need to live by the rules, but especially black Americans. We need to prepare the kids for the 21st century. Without our efforts now, we'll lose another generation. And we, the black race, cannot afford to lose another generation. We can't afford to lose another child. We need to be sure that all our children will be prepared for the life that awaits them. This means we need to be involved in their lives and their schooling. We need to be concerned about how they're doing in school. We need to meet with their teachers to ensure they are attending and studying hard. And we need to let them know that we are checking on them. We also need teachers to inform us as parents of the progress our kids are making—or not making. I know teachers have a big job keeping up with lesson plans and maintaining their students' interest. But we need to require them to do just a little more. A simple form letter could be mailed to the parents' office (never to the home, because kids can and will intercept letters mailed to the home), stating that their son or daughter seems to be having problems with certain subjects and asking them to please contact the school to arrange an appointment. This would alert the parents of any potential problems so they could help head them off. We as parents must be willing

87

to follow through with meeting teachers and counselors to discuss these problems.

It all starts with you as parents and filters down to your children. If your kids see you calling in sick when you're not, why wouldn't they believe they can do likewise? When they hear you telling how you take advantage of your position on the job, you better believe they will decide to find ways to take advantage at school.

We need to be aware that our actions will be reflected in how our kids will live their lives. So, as parents, we must at all times be on our best behavior—for the preparation of the kids.

A Subjective Subject Ranking

1. **History:** Because history repeats itself, the lessons it teaches will be valuable for your participation in the Game. You must learn the history of America and its people in order not to make the mistakes others have already made. Although your history classes may seem boring and stupid, keep in mind that someday what you are learning may help you through a problem or a rough time.

2. **English:** Remember, the white man controls how life in this country operates. Your job is to find and define your place in this world. Your mastery of the English language

will make this job a lot easier, as it will ensure that you can communicate with the white man on his level.

3. **Math:** You need a knowledge of math to be able to manage the money you earn while playing the Game. You also need math to perform most jobs available in the playing field.

4. **Economics:** You need to understand how the economy affects the money you earn and how to make the most of the news you hear about the economy. You also need to be able to understand the tax laws and codes.

5. **Civics:** Understanding how the government operates and how it affects your life is essential. You should learn your rights under the Constitution and the proper legal methods to effect change.

6. **Physical Education:** You must keep your body in top shape, along with your mind.

7. **All other elective subjects offered in school:** You need these to become a well-rounded person and be a productive member of society.

89

A community that allows...young men to grow up in broken families, dominated by women, never acquiring any stable relationship to male authority...asks for and gets chaos.... Crime, violence, unrest, unrestrained lashing out...are not only expected, they are very nearly inevitable.

—Senator Daniel Patrick Moynihan

The Winning Attitude

Improve your attitude.

Reject the idea that the white man is out
to keep the black man down. By playing
the blame game, we do nothing to improve
our status and pass on nothing of value to
our children. We must develop an attitude
of continual self-improvement—in the
workplace and in our neighborhoods.

I live my life in the white man's world. My work and recreational lives are spent with him. I have only a couple of black friends, and they, too, live and work in the white man's world. This situation has not arisen by choice. It has happened because my job very seldom deals with black businesses, nor do I live in a black-populated area.

I don't know if this is good or bad. It's just the way it is. The white man's way of life is the one I grew up observing and studying. I don't wish to sound as if I'm trying to be white or that I'm telling you that the white man's way of life is the right way. The way I choose to live is my decision and the way you choose is your decision.

I don't expect all black men to adopt the white man's way of life, but I think it's obvious we need to try something different. I have such contempt for the way the black man lives his life and then complains how it is playing

93

out. We must all find our own way. It all comes down to attitude. My reason for writing this guide is to let the brothers know there is something more to life than drugs, gangs, and handouts. There's a whole world waiting for you to make your mark on it.

Let's get off the street corners and show the younger brothers the way things should be. Let's dissolve the gangs and provide safe communities for our children. Let's have willpower and become leaders rather than followers.

Driving through just about any urban black neighborhood in the United States, you'll see businesses mostly gone, storefronts boarded up, trash in the streets, unkempt yards, and always the favorite corner hangout. This is the same type of neighborhood I grew up in and where I heard all too frequently how the white man was holding our race back, how we could accomplish nothing because the white man made sure there was nothing for us. There *was* nothing for us, not on those corners.

We have a long way to go to understand what it takes to keep a race strong. The white man knows. Look at the big difference between how he does things and how we do things.

You call me brother to my face, but as soon

as my back is turned you're planning how to steal my possessions. You observe me to find what you can steal from me, not to learn how I got it. We prey upon each other more than any other race in America. And it is this kind of attitude that destroys a race from within.

The legislative, legal, and educational systems in this country are all available to us, but it's up to us to take advantage of them. We can always find someone to blame, but generally, in today's society, we have to take responsibility for what happens when we don't educate ourselves and try to jump in the Game. It's easy to blame the white man, but you can't lie to yourself.

Can we take a hint from other minorities who help one another, such as the American Koreans, the American Jews, the American Chinese, the American Cubans, and the American Italians? They patronize each other's businesses. They respect each other's possessions. They teach their people to play the Game and win. I'm not saying these groups don't have their problems, but more than likely they are united in the belief that education and hard work are the key to making it in this country. The black race does not see it that way.

Have we lost the morals our forefathers maintained even in slavery? Their leaders

95

were moral leaders; without their influence, Lord knows where our race would be today. These are the people our children need to hear about, but you can't teach what you yourself don't know. We search back through history for evidence of how the white man oppressed us, but not of what our own ancestors endured to make our life livable. Of course there were those who wished to rise up and seize their freedom. The leaders who saw beyond revenge were the ones who had the good of the entire race in mind. They are my role models. Without them, my life would be drastically different. I thank them for maintaining the morals of our race and making sure I was able to pass these principles on to the next generation. You need to rediscover those morals yourself and pass them on to your children.

I cringe each time I hear about the latest murder or drive-by shooting. Does it take a genius to see that we are only hurting ourselves? No one cares if blacks kill blacks. It's only when blacks kill others that it becomes a national outrage. Black people must learn that the only people who care what happens in the black neighborhoods of our cities are the blacks who live there. Most blacks who live outside those neighborhoods have no interest in life there; they have the same attitude as the white man: Let those people do as they please as long as they do it to each other.

That was my attitude, too, until I realized that everything that happened in those neighborhoods also hurt me. Because of stereotyping, I am perceived to be the same as any other black man on the street. I've had to deal with starting a new job and overcoming coworkers' preconceptions of me. White people in the workplace have said to me, "You're not like most of the black people I've met." I'm always at a loss as to how to respond. Do I thank them? Do I take offense? Do I ask what they mean?

> White people in the workplace have said to me, "You're not like most of the black people I've met." I'm always at a loss as to how to respond. Do I thank them? Do I take offense? Do I ask what they mean?

We must ask ourselves why we are the most negatively stereotyped people in America. It's because we always fulfill the white man's expectations. The white man expects us to be lazy and depend upon him, and we do. He expects us to have no family values, no morals, no respect for one another, and we don't. The white man doesn't need to work at figuring out what the black man's next move will be. He has only to expect it to happen, and we will oblige.

We have no pride in ourselves as a race. We have no pride in the accomplishments of

97

our forefathers. When did we lose all the black pride that was expressed in the '60s and '70s? A black man in today's society can do and be anything he wishes if he takes the initiative.

The welfare system was set up for those needing a helping hand. It was not set up to provide a living for the black race. Don't you want more from life than a handout? Think how proud you'll feel knowing you have done something for yourself. Think how gratified you'll feel when your kids run up to you with their big smiles, confident that you are taking care of them. Think how good you'll feel to have a life instead of just an existence. There are no limits to what you can accomplish.

Let us band together and go down in history as the generation who cared enough for the children and future generations to make the change.

You think the more children you have and don't take care of is a badge of pride? If it is, it's only because we have boasted to the younger brothers time and time again that it is. Our job is to provide the leadership and instead show them the proper way to live. We need to teach the next generation to keep the race strong. We need to teach them to keep the family intact or our race will fade away.

We need to consider the consequences of living our lives in a disrespectful manner. I

98

hate to walk down the street and see white people clutching at their belongings in fear simply because I'm black. I hate to see young black men gathering to cause trouble. I hate to see the lack of pride in the race. I hate to see gangs taking over the neighborhoods and spreading fear among their own people.

Why do we, as a race, feel the need to destroy everything related to the American way of life? Do we have such resentment for it? Can we still blame the white man for the actions of his ancestors? The black people who have gotten beyond the hatred and the blame are the ones who have won the Game. Let's become American first, interacting with other Americans, be they white, Asian, or whatever.

As I drive through a black inner-city neighborhood and see the lack of care, I think, We need to change this. It would be nice to see businesses thriving, and all the people of the community working together. It would be nice to see life there as I see it in other neighborhoods.

If we start to change our ways, how people perceive us will change, too. Nothing will improve until others' perceptions of the black race change. And we're the only ones who can effect that change. I try to do my part every day. I make sure to overturn the stereotypes of

99

blacks with every white person I meet. But it takes more than just one or two or even a million—it takes the entire black race. Let us come together and make that change.

Consider these as a basis for change:

• Change from the street-corner drug dealer to the legitimate salesman.

• Change from the pimp in the Cadillac to the brother with the right stuff.

• Change from the career criminal to having a career.

• Change from the gang member to the family member.

• Change from the absentee father to the father who's there for his kids.

Our children must be taught the Declaration of Independence and how its promise of life, liberty, and the pursuit of happiness applies to them as well. The only way to teach them this is to live it. Those of us who are hardworking and who provide well for our families must be the role models for our race, to convince our children that this is how life should be.

We must teach the children to dream, and show them that their dreams can be achieved. We cannot afford to lose another generation. It is up to us, black men between the ages of 25 and 45. The burden of proof has been set upon our shoulders.

Many of our kids are learning that the only way to get anything out of life is to steal it. We must change this way of thinking, and take back our kids and our communities from the gangs. Hard work and dedication to family are what must be taught.

The current generation must reject the idea that the white man is out to get us, that there is a conspiracy to keep the black man down. We must reject the idea that our opportunity to make it depends on someone other than us. We must not expect that the government will take care of us, that the welfare system is a way to make a living. It is there to help honest, hardworking people who have had a run of bad luck, or people with mental and physical problems. We owe nothing to those who have repeatedly abused the system.

Our negative, defeatist attitudes have got us stuck. We can't continue to pass them onto our children. The chain must be broken right here and right now.

For black role models who have won at the Game to come into the neighborhoods and talk about how they've succeeded is almost worthless if a child's daily role models are the neighborhood's human debris. Without change from the inside, there will never be a mass exodus of black people from poverty.

101

We need at least to offer the next generation a chance at their dreams. Let them take
advantage of the opportunities afforded them,
to make the choices we should have made.
Give them the chance to educate themselves
and, in turn, help make a change in their
neighborhoods, their families, themselves.

Parents must teach their children that sex
is something to be saved until marriage or at
least until they are mature enough to handle
the responsibility that comes along with it.
The black man must model this attitude.
He must no longer father children and leave
the responsibility to the mother. Do your part,
brothers. Older brother teaching younger
brother, father teaching son, one kid breaking
the chain.

This chain links all of us together as a
stereotype, not as a race. We must break the
chain in order to become the race of people
we want to be. Those who have played the
Game and succeeded should be proud of
their accomplishments. The brothers who
call them the sellouts and Toms should be
ashamed because they chose not to educate
themselves and strive for a better life than the
one their parents had.

We must change in order to save our race.
Let us band together and go down in history
as the generation who cared enough for the

children and future generations. I have already begun simply by teaching my son how life should be lived. If all the brothers teach at least one younger brother how to win the Game and attain the life he's dreamed about, we can turn things around quickly and all have better lives.

We must assume our responsibilities like the men we were meant to be. Let go of the fear that others will bad-mouth you. As your life changes for the better, this will bother you less and less. When you see what you can accomplish, nothing the brothers on the corner say will make you want to return to the life you had there. And, by changing your attitude and being motivated to make the change, you will have forged a link in a strong black chain.

Beyond Goals to Aspirations

Have we no pride in ourselves? Do we want nothing from life? Can we continue to blame all that is wrong with our lives on the white man? Let us take the blame for the things that are wrong with our race. Let our children not have to look to television and to the stadiums and ballparks for role models. They should look to their parents to teach them the lessons they need: to have pride and confidence that they can do anything.

103

Can we do this? Sure we can. But it will take the efforts of all of us to instill these values in our children; not just your children, but also the children of your neighbors and friends. The teachings must spread from your children to their friends and peers. We must all agree that this will lead to a better life for the children and for us, too.

Life isn't so long that you and I may see a change in how we are perceived by the white man, but the effort has to start sometime. It matters less that we see the change than we create the foundation for change. The efforts we put forth now will be enjoyed by our children and our children's children.

The efforts of the race are what make it strong. Rid yourselves of the notion that the world is here for you and only for you. Think of the brothers who will follow. Think of the world you will leave to them. Think, brothers, think...

I remember seeing the brothers hanging on the corners, leaving the bars drunk on their ass, arriving home and abusing their wives and kids to no end. I thought, This is not the life I want to lead. One positive thing I got from them was a statement one of them made to me as I was about to tell him my goals in life: "Keep your goals to yourself, because once you share your goals, they become challenges." I interpreted this statement to mean that as long as you're the only one who knows your goals, you have nothing to prove to anyone but yourself. Your goals should be just that, your goals.

However, after experiencing life as I have, I no longer have goals—I have aspirations. The very idea of a goal establishes a stopping point. But aspirations have no limitations, because you can always aspire to do better.

When people ask me what I wish from life, my answer is always, "I want it all." And I don't believe there is anything in life I want that I will not achieve.

We must believe that there is a better life for us and a way to achieve that life. It takes respecting one another. It takes us showing we love our community and our race. It takes accepting responsibility for our actions. It takes stopping the glorification of things we know to be wrong. It takes shattering the stereotypes of our race. It takes dreaming and acting on those dreams. It takes motivation. It takes a lot of heart. It takes courage. It takes the right attitude.

Chapter Six

There is a mountain of...evidence showing that when families disintegrate, children... end up with...scars that persist for life...

—Karl Zinmeister, American Enterprise Institute

The Home Court:
Family and Community

Develop your moral ethics.

The white man plays the Game because
he wants to provide—emotionally and
financially—for his children, and this
inspires them. The black man must
become an excellent role model for
his children as well.

107

I t begins and ends in the home. All parents must consider the lives of the children they bring into this world. Our kids cannot be frightened of failure or of the possibility that not all their dreams will come true. They must be encouraged to continue dreaming, and they must have self-esteem and confidence in how strong they are. They'll learn soon enough that life is hard, but they must also learn that a strong person can make it through. Children must understand that hard work and commitment will increase their chances for success. And it must be stressed that this begins with the education they receive when they are young, maximized by their willingness to work hard and their motivation to succeed. If a child sees adults building a better life, he or she will be motivated to also strive to build a better one.

Blacks who realize success in the Game

109

should be willing to help those who are not as successful. And they, in turn, must show they deserve the help that successful blacks are willing to give. To deserve that help, we must lose the chip on our shoulders, open our minds, and express the desire for something better for our families. We must admit that we have problems and be ready to solve those problems.

I've heard the claims that the justice system is unfair to blacks. There's a simple way to avoid unfair treatment by the justice system: Don't commit a crime.

A big problem with the black neighborhood is that *it's the black neighborhood.* Black people must understand that by congregating in only one or two areas of a city, as we usually do, we alienate ourselves from the rest of the populace. The white man wants this to happen because it minimizes the effort of focusing his watchful eye upon us. We have to diversify where we live in order to learn more about winning the Game.

To succeed in the Game, we need to learn about other cultures. Proximity to other races and cultures will allow us the opportunity to observe and ask about their lives. How do their problems compare to ours? How do they handle these problems? Where do they go for help when they need it? How do parents motivate their children? We can discover

110

different ways of doing things without losing our own culture or identity. No matter what you do in life, believe me, you will always be a black American.

Let us pass the idea of helping each other on to the children so that they pass it on to their children and so on. Remember the days when people helped bear one another's burdens? When family members had a place to go and someone to take care of them? People cared about the kids in the neighborhood. Even the fellows on the corner had a place in their hearts for the kids. If people in the neighborhood saw us doing something we shouldn't, they stepped in and stopped us. I can remember pleading with them not to tell my great-grandmother about something bad I did, but they always would. They told me that one day I'd thank them for what they did for me. And today I do.

Communities must come together to clean up the neighborhoods. Make the neighborhoods look decent, and decent attitudes will prevail. A clean neighborhood shows you have the entire community's best interest at heart.

We commit crimes against one another more than any other race in America. Why? Why must we be afraid to leave our homes? Why do we allow gangs to rule our neighborhoods? Why do we protect the criminals of

111

our race from suffering the consequences they deserve? We have a justice system to deal with people who disobey the law. It doesn't matter what race a person is: Justice is administered for crimes against society—not for being a member of an individual race.

I've heard the claims that the justice system is unfair to blacks, that blacks can always expect worse treatment than whites. There's a simple way to avoid unfair treatment by the justice system: Don't commit a crime. If the energy you put into planning a crime went instead toward finding a decent job and supporting your family, you'd be miles ahead.

Helping the people next door when they are in trouble will come back to you when you need help. Don't turn your back on the brother who asks for help. But as you offer help, keep these thoughts in mind: Give a man a fish and feed him for a day, but teach him to fish and feed him for life. Never give a handout, but always give a hand. When you help another member of your race, you ultimately help yourself.

A good way to begin would be to patronize black-owned and black-managed businesses, including those in outlying areas. Research those black-owned businesses that sell or provide the services you seek and then patronize them. Ask to meet the black owners and managers of businesses you research. Introduce yourself and, if the services and products are satisfactory, inform them that you will be back and that you will recommend the business to your friends. The one thing that will ensure the success of a black-owned business is to have blacks patronize it.

If this catches on, more and more black businesses will become successful, and more and more blacks will, too. The

The one thing that will ensure the success of a black-owned business is to have blacks patronize it. This is not a new idea, as the Jewish and the Asian communities, and especially the white community, have followed this practice for as long as business has existed.

benefits will spread throughout the community in the form of more jobs and a more stable business environment, increased competition and lower prices for goods, and successful role models for the children and more opportunities for their future.

This is not a new idea, as the Jewish and the Asian communities, and especially the white community, have followed this practice for as long as business has existed. While the black community is not unaware of the practice, black patrons often don't ensure their dollars go to one of their own. We in the black community are usually the last to capitalize on

113

certain concepts, business or otherwise. To improve, we need to watch and learn from other races.

Black businesses need to do their part as well, by encouraging blacks to apply for jobs in their establishments. We need not show favoritism, but with large numbers of blacks to apply for positions, the owners should have no problem finding the right people for the jobs. Begin by giving a kid in the neighborhood a chance before advertising citywide for the job.

The kids should not just be given a job. They should also be taught how the workplace functions. Be sure that the help you offer will enable the person to transfer skills and apply them when the opportunity arises.

Unfortunately, because of negative stereotypes, successful black businesses have always been reluctant to hire neighborhood blacks. We have joked about these stereotypes for so long that we've begun to believe them ourselves. It doesn't take much for a black person to believe the worst about other blacks, and this, too, is tearing us apart.

We have to change the negative perceptions, and start an affirmative action program for our own communities. Let's not wait to hire the brightest black kids coming out of

114

college. These are not the kids who need our help. They will be sought after by the white man, as they'll be looked upon as players in the Game. The local black businesses need to offer a chance to the kids who need to be saved from the ways of the streets. Unless we provide them an alternative, they will become our future criminals and drag us down.

The kids should not just be given a job. They should also be taught how the workplace functions. Having any job may keep them off the streets and out of trouble for a while. But what happens when they leave the security of your little nest, thinking that they have some skills to offer the work world, and find out that the only reason they were kept on was that you felt sorry for them? Their confidence will be shattered. Their trust in employers will be shaken. You will have hurt them more than you helped. Be sure that the help you offer will enable the person to transfer skills and apply them when the opportunity arises.

Kids need help to learn how to prepare for the Game. They need to be confident when applying for jobs. They need to see people in their own communities as positive role models living the American dream so they can learn from them. They need to see a future for themselves. They need to feel loved—not just by their parents but by their entire community.

They need to know that their family extends to all corners of their neighborhood and they can go outside without fear.

Our kids must be taught how to take control of their lives. They must understand that the blame game no longer works. White Americans today are no longer willing to pay restitution for the oppression of black people by yesterday's racist white America.

If the help does not come from the parents, the community leaders, and the role models, we will continue to lose our kids to the streets. Let our generation be the one that made the change to save the children of our race. Let us go down in history as a generation of something other than killers and gang members.

It's our job to be there for our kids, to offer role models and firm, clear guidance. Strong family and community values are the roots of change in our race. Open your eyes and look around you. See the many black people playing and winning the Game. Understand the road they chose. Look down that road and meet the challenge. Forget the jeers and sneers from the losers on the corner and be your own man, the black man you were born to be, the black man who has the right role models and who will someday be a role model to others. Be a link in the strong black chain of future generations. The chain cannot handle one weak link. It requires nothing but strong black men willing to change our race for the better.

Just'us

You know the old saying WHAT DOES JUSTICE MEAN TO A BLACK MAN? JUST US. The justice system has been hard on blacks. But the blame belongs with blacks. We've used all the excuses we can for why we steal, rape, and kill. But the truth is we have no respect for our people. Kids are killing kids for the sheer pleasure of it. As fast as they lock up one black male, another takes his place. And we blame the white man for it, saying "We are killing each other because the white man has kept us down for so long."

The fact is, the white man doesn't care if blacks kill blacks. Let's take a little history lesson and see what we haven't learned. In the days of slavery, the white man could get away with beating, raping, and killing blacks. The white man lacked respect for blacks and devalued them, believing them to be less than human. Today, blacks try to get away with beating, raping, and killing blacks. We lack respect for our brothers and sisters, we devalue them. It's history repeating itself in a tragic way.

117

The point is that we have turned the hatred heaped upon us by the white man against our own people. We are responsible for how we conduct ourselves and our own lives. We need to understand that we are the shapers of our destiny.

We, as a race, are represented in the prison system in large numbers. But we have also committed crimes in large numbers. I've heard about the white man keeping us in poverty, which causes us to turn to crime in order to survive. Poverty isn't what makes us commit crimes. A lack of morals and respect for others and their belongings is what makes us commit crimes. The black criminal preys primarily on other blacks. Gang violence explodes primarily in and around the gang members' neighborhoods.

Why do we feel such desire to take what others have? Why do we resist working for things? We argue that the white man has kept us down for so long that this is our only revenge. Let's think about this. To exact our revenge for the white man's forefathers' treatment of our forefathers, we destroy our own neighborhoods and kill our own people? This makes perfect sense! I understand it now! We'll teach the white man a lesson by killing our own people, and those who aren't dead will be in prison.

Haven't we figured out that the only ones being hurt are blacks? Our kids are dying in the streets, our families and neighborhoods are breaking down, too many of our strong young brothers are in prison, and we feel we have harmed the white man.

We need to teach the kids how to stay out of prison, not how to get away with crimes. This is something parents must teach at home. It's better not to be in prison when trying to teach your kids to live a law-abiding life.

We must teach our kids that for those who choose to disobey the law, they and they alone are responsible for the consequences. It is not the white man or the government or society that has dealt them the hand they are playing. They have dealt it to themselves.

Chapter Seven

I'm sick and tired of black and white people of good intent giving aspirin to a society that is dying of a cancerous disease.

—Reverend Ralph D. Abernathy

The Rule Makers: Political Agendas

Become self-sufficient.

Government programs such as welfare only keep us dependent on white policy makers. Handouts aren't really free, and they will never expand your mind the way education and self-motivation will.

121

Because blacks receive a welfare check, they think they are politically active. There is a lot more to being politically active than having the government manage your life! And welfare was never meant to be a career.

Everyone in my neighborhood had an opinion about politics, but few actually knew whereof they spoke. I remember them saying the government controlled the lives of people on welfare. Friends would complain how government intervention had screwed up their lives. But how can you avoid government intervention when your life is dependent upon the government? You control how involved the government is in your life by your dependence upon it for your income, as well as your aspirations in life.

I consider myself to be a political conservative, although I don't follow such views blindly.

123

I don't wish to dictate how people should live, but when their lifestyle affects me, particularly my wallet, I feel it's time for me to speak up. The way I look at it is, your reluctance to work and provide for your family is akin to stealing from me—a kind of legal stealing, with the government as an accomplice. Your inability to provide for your family and insistence that the government do so means that I am taxed to make that possible. I hate to think of myself as uncaring and lacking in compassion, but there is a point where charity stops and the well-being of my family takes precedence—particularly since no one can take care of my family as well as I can.

The government can never do as much for you as you can do for yourself.

If someone becomes complacent with the government's handouts, they will become totally dependent upon them. The purpose of government should not be to provide handouts to people. In fact, the more handouts the government provides, the less energy and funds it has to devote to its true purpose: to protect the country and its allies, and to maintain and operate the nation's infrastructure. And taxpayers are becoming more and more angry with funding the abuse of a system that was created to help people in need until they are able to return to the workforce.

124

Opponents of reform are correct when they contend that children receive the greatest amount of welfare funds. But to those who argue that the kids will suffer if the system is changed, I counter that my kids will suffer if it isn't. Every cent I am taxed to pay for the welfare system is a cent taken from my kids.

I know this problem isn't as simple as I'm making it out to be. But I've heard enough from the people who make their living from welfare; it's time they heard from us, the taxpayers. We carry the load they refuse to. It's not my fault that they decided not to educate themselves. They chose their life, and bringing kids into a world they themselves resent is unforgivable. The welfare recipient learns how the system works and how to beat it: have more kids. While I realize that not all people on welfare take advantage of the system, many do. It's fine for someone who is healthy and able to work to choose not to—until the government mandates that we be taxed to support them.

125

The government can never do as much for you as you can do for yourself. Everyone must do their best to become self-reliant. You will never regret the effort you make to achieve your dreams.

One of the government's programs is affirmative action. When it was put into place, it was 'the only way to break through the good ol' boy network and it offered blacks and other minorities the chance to prove themselves in the workplace. We've always said that all we needed was the chance to prove what we can do. Well, we've been given that chance, and the white man is still waiting for most of us to prove ourselves on the job. We've proven that we can manipulate the system to our advantage, that we can complain about everything that isn't perfect about our lives. I think it's time we prove that we can do the job we begged so hard for the chance to do.

Forget the idea that you will be welcomed with open arms in a new workplace. You must be ready to deal with animosity. Enter cautiously and aim to prove the naysayers wrong. Your focus must never waver, your motivation to be the best can never weaken. As your abilities increase, you will impress your coworkers and supervisors, and you'll earn their respect. Demonstrate your talent for your chosen career. When you deal with the white man on his level, you will be amazed at the amount of respect you get from him. Remember, respect is something you have to earn.

The first thing a businessperson must think about is the company and its profits. Without profits, there is no company, and without a company, there are no workers. A business has no obligation to hire you just because you show up on its doorstep, and the government was not designed to oversee which candidates a business hires. Investors don't sit down to form a business plan just because they feel the need to provide jobs for certain people. But that is just what the government does, and because it can't create jobs for all the people it determines need them, it mandates existing businesses to hire these people through affirmative action.

The black race has endured a lot of racism and discrimination, but a government mandate that employers hire minorities is not the only answer. Trying to be the best person for the job is also the answer.

When you apply for a job, and the interviewer is white and the other applicants are white, you probably feel you have little chance of getting the position. But black people can and should most definitely take advantage of affirmative action, especially if it is the only way to break into the career they choose. I'd like to think I've never benefited from affirmative action, but I can't be sure. What's detrimental about affirmative action is that sometimes people are retained in positions they can't handle, and their coworkers are aware of it. They wonder why one person

127

should be favored over another because of his skin color.

Imagine yourself as a black businessman deciding between two candidates for a job in your company: one of them black, the other white. The white candidate has five years' real-work experience in the position, and the black candidate has only a little experience. Which candidate do you hire? These are the considerations you must weigh: What is in the company's best interest? Do I hire someone who lacks experience but meets the government's quota? Do I have the time to train someone for the job? How much productivity will be lost for the company if I hire the less experienced worker? What will other employees think of me and their new, inexperienced coworker? Do I hire the white person over the black even though I am black? You might try prioritizing these issues, highlighting the interests of the company and the qualifications of the candidate. You will want to be sure during the job interview to assess the personalities and attitudes of the candidates as well as their work experience. This is not affirmative action, it is good business sense. Think about it.

The black race has endured a lot of racism and discrimination, but a government mandate that employers hire minorities is not the only answer. Trying to be the best person for the job is also the answer.

The Constitution is a pretty good affirmative action policy. The only problem is that we have been relaxed in enforcing it and instead have been guided by policies created by emotional public debates.

—Congressman J.C. Watts

The founding fathers did not establish our government to regulate the country's wealth. Opportunities abound in any field you wish to pursue. In order to obtain wealth, you must do one of two things: either inherit it or educate yourself and work hard. The best route is to rely on your own resources and work long and hard to achieve your dreams. Blacks have a bad habit of waiting for things to come to them and then complaining that what they receive is too little.

Get for yourself what you wish, and if it's not enough, you can work for more. This is what makes America great. The opportunities are there, but until you make your own way, you'll be dependent upon the government to provide you with your life.

As Americans, we have the power to vote. This gives us the chance to elect leaders who can help us help ourselves. We don't need leaders to go to Washington and bring back more handout programs. Our leaders must understand the problems of the inner city and provide solutions that work. We need to look beyond the color of the candidate and study

129

the platform he runs on and how it will help the race overall. Rate the person first, then his platform.

Blacks must ask more from our politicians. We need to be sure that their ideas and values will benefit our children and the generations to come. We need to be sure of their commitment to change the attitudes of the black race and not just bring more social programs to our communities. We don't need more programs; we need more positive attitudes and role models.

We don't need more handouts or affirmative action programs. We need real change in our attitudes and the attitudes of our leaders.

We need to hold the national black leaders' feet to the fire and get them to provide us with what we need to help ourselves: better schools and teachers to educate our children, better policing for our neighborhoods, better opportunities for the community. We don't need more handouts or affirmative action programs. We need real change in our attitudes and the attitudes of our leaders.

We must remember that the leaders we send to Washington are no better than we are. If we live our lives in a manner that is right and good, then and only then can we expect the leaders we elect to live up to those standards. Our behavior and attitudes will shape those not only of current black leaders, but ultimately of the black leaders of the future.

We have lost the belief that in America we can do and be anything we wish, and instead we play the blame game: Our kids' problems are the fault of the government for not providing enough programs to keep them off the streets. Our problems are the fault of the government for not creating enough jobs we can perform. Our neighborhoods' problems are the fault of the government for neglecting the inner city's black communities. These are just a few of our excuses for not pursuing the American dream.

The reality is that it is not the job of the government to keep your kids off the streets. That responsibility falls directly on your shoulders as their parents. Your kids are the way they are because they are emulating the way you're living. It is not the job of the government to create work for the people of this country who choose not to educate themselves or train for a career. You are the way you are because you choose to be that way. It is not solely the job of the government to ensure the safety of your neighborhoods. You must bring up your kids with good morals and values, and teach them to respect the lives and possessions of your neighbors, and take pride in the community. Have some pride in yourself

131

and your race. Look to yourself for the things you want from life.

It doesn't matter how much money you provide for a neighborhood if the attitudes of the people in the neighborhood don't change. It doesn't matter how many programs you set up if people lack the motivation to take advantage of them. It doesn't matter how many jobs you create for blacks if the blacks don't want them. The policy of giving a handout for a certain period of time has turned into a way of life for a lot of black Americans.

There are those who are subsidized by our tax dollars who are addicted to drugs and alcohol, and they use the handouts to maintain their lifestyle of addiction. As one recipient said, "It's better I receive this money this way than being on the street, robbing people for it." It's still robbery, whether it's done by the individual or the government on behalf of the individual. This idea of just throwing money at all the problems we have in society must be looked at seriously. It's difficult for hardworking people to be the best they can be with someone in addition to their family to support.

The Peanut Analogy

To set the stage for the peanut analogy we need to know the characters:

- You, or the Many—the black man, or the black race
- The Man—the white man, or the white race
- The Few—the black leaders
- The Hole—the bottom rung of the ladder
- Education—the hand to help you out of the Hole
- The Peanut—money or success
- The Program—the welfare system

The Many start in the Hole, not knowing the Peanut is there for them to pursue because they're taught that it is to be provided by the Man. The Man started the Program, thinking that providing the Peanut was the helping the Many needed. But as the Program grew and developed, the Man began to realize his mistake. He never foresaw that the Program would become a way of life for some and a way to abuse the system for others. By this time, it was too late to end or even alter the Program, lest the Man be called racist and uncaring.

Then a flash of brilliance: The Man would educate a few of the Many to teach the others how to provide for themselves. However, the Few soon discovered that being the providers of the Peanuts enabled them to oversee the allotment of Peanuts, and with no supervision from the Man (why would the Man think the

133

Few would steal from their own people?), the Few had every opportunity to skim any amount they wished from the total. And the more the Few educated themselves, the more they realized how much they could benefit by manipulating the Many. This included lying about the amount of allotted Peanuts and the restrictions the Man enforced on these allotments. The Few soon had the Many as dependent upon them as they were upon the Man.

Another mistake by the Man—instead of educating the Many, he chose to educate the Few and let the Many learn by example. The Few soon learned to live the good life at the expense of the Many. Every so often the Few assured the Many that they were working hard to convince the Man to educate them all. But this wasn't true, for to educate the Many—to teach them to take full advantage of the system set up by the Man—jeopardizes the easy life the Few enjoy. And the Many fear actually trying to do for themselves and not relying on the Few to provide for them. As long as the Many remain dependent on the Few, and the Many and the Man have no access to each other except through the Few, nothing will change.

In a perfect world, the Man's plan would have worked, with the Many following the lead of the Few and educating themselves. Or, in the beginning, had he only given the Many the tools to educate themselves and not the Peanuts by way of the Program, they would be better off today.

Well, that's it in a nutshell. The message is: Take the hand of the Man, climb out of the Hole, and start to educate yourselves. There probably won't be more opportunities for the Many than there are now. Don't be content with just Peanuts from the Few. Think of how your life can change if you just apply yourself. Let's be prepared to help one another and benefit ourselves—starting today.

135

Any man, regardless of color, will be recognized and rewarded in proportion as he learns to do something well, learns to do it better than anyone else, however humble.

—Booker T. Washington

136

The Future

The Game is never over.

Whether you are part of it or not,
the Game continues.

137

Whites and blacks need to take responsibility for the problems they've caused: The white man has sought to oppress, and the black man has made himself easy to oppress. The black man needs to learn the system and take advantage of its social and economic programs. He must find the genuine desire to turn his back on handouts and instead reach for the helping hand that will enable him to raise himself out of poverty. He must take the initiative and show he has the drive to work for what he wants in life.

It seems at times that as far as the black race is concerned, the dream of the pursuit of happiness has been lost. We spend so much time blaming others for our problems, but until we look to ourselves for the solutions to our problems, we can never be assured of being happy. We have to do for ourselves.

139

I hope that my son will have a better life than mine, a life that is color-blind. I hope he is looked at not as a minority, but as an American putting his best foot forward.

If the black man begins to realize the power of education, the road to success is endless. If our race is to survive, this message must be conveyed to the younger generation. The number of kids who drop out of the public school system is overwhelming. We put ads on television and radio to convince them to stay in school, but they see their parents in dead-end jobs from the lack of education, and the message doesn't get through. If we, as parents, fail to point the kids in the right direction, we have lost. Don't be ashamed to admit to your kids that you've made mistakes. And don't make another one by complaining to them that the white man held you back.

If the black man begins to realize the power of education, the road to success is endless.

We need to make Hollywood—both black and white—take more responsibility for the movies it gives us and to use the media to communicate positive messages. We, as parents, must recognize the power and influence they have over the youth of this country. Movies so cheapen life that the killings on our streets each day mean nothing. Movies and TV shows are not to blame for society's problems, but things may be better if they were another source of positive role models. The "blaxploitation films" of the 1970s—*Shaft, Superfly, Cleopatra Jones,* and any movie with Fred Williamson—glorified drug dealers, abusers of women, and taking from the white man. We were supposed to root for the "hero" to get the girl and the money at the end.

I keep waiting for positive messages to come from Spike Lee, Mario Van Peebles, and other black producers and directors. But all we get is the same old thing from the '70s: Black is good and white is bad. Is this all we can expect from the black Hollywood elite? Don't they recognize the opportunity they have to lead our race down another road? Maybe they feel it's no longer their problem since they've "made it." It's the peanut analogy at work.

I hope that blacks will cease committing crimes against whites and other blacks. I also hope that animosity between the races finally ends. I hope that the KKK and other white-supremacist groups will be suppressed and that people learn to live together. Diversity is what this country was built on. Once you get past the physical differences, you tend to find that we all have the same dreams and aspirations. I hope that someday we will live as

141

Americans in America, not as blacks, whites, Asians, Hispanics, and Jews.

I hope that black neighborhoods will finally have the same economic opportunities as other neighborhoods enjoy, and that blacks begin to feel the same pride in their neighborhoods as others do. I hope that business and community leaders will help the children achieve their dreams. I hope they will actively involve themselves in the lives of our kids. These leaders, and not the drug dealers and gang leaders, are the people our young children should strive to emulate.

As parents, we must make sure the kids see us living right. Most experts tell us that the rise of gangs stems from the breakup of the family unit, the increasing number of single-parent homes, the loss of self-esteem in the black community, and the lack of other opportunities for young black men. The family unit is the core of society. We, the black race, have lost all family values, along with the will to regain them. Brothers are still fathering kids, without regard for how those kids will turn out or the life they'll have. It may not always be an ideal situation when the father is in the home, but our family unit must be what changes us. In the days of slavery, the family unit kept our people going. Whether it was the need to be reunited or the desire to keep the family together at all costs, this was their daily existence.

Look at how the black race lives in this country: roaming the streets at night to prey upon the vulnerable, stealing and foraging for what they need to get by, fathering kids with no regard for their care and no thought or feeling for their mothers, caring only about themselves and not the race as a whole, providing no value whatsoever to society. We are essentially living like the cavemen, barely distinguishable from animals.

I hope that we will have the courage to treat criminals as criminals and not as victims of the justice system. The blame for the crimes committed by these people should be placed directly on them. I think that, basically, criminals commit crimes because it is the easiest way to get what they want, and they need to be held accountable for their crimes. We don't need to build more prisons. We need to stop the madness that is creating more criminals.

143

If you chose not to prepare yourself for the Game, be a man about it and tell the kids the truth. Stop telling the lie that the white man has somehow done something to hold you down. Equip your kids with the knowledge that no man, black or white, is better or more capable than they are. This is the attitude we must convey to them through our actions and our very lives.

I hope that we will make a difference in the lives of the younger generation, enabling them to take advantage of all that is there for them. I hope this guide gives the younger brothers an idea of the paths they should follow. This is the key to the black race surviving in the white man's world.

I lay down a challenge here and now to all brothers to go out and help our kids down a better road to a better life. The things we thought were so far away would then be within their reach. I lay this same challenge to my son, to live his life the right way and to show those behind him how life should be lived.

The American dream is out there, and it's ours for the taking.

144

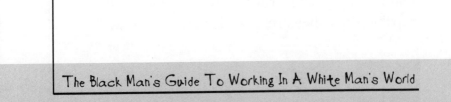